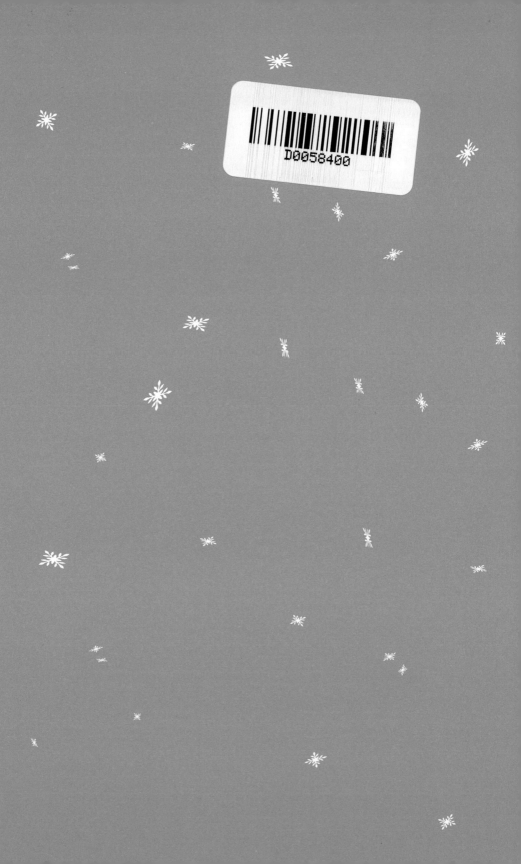

DO TEDDY BEARS SKI?

Mountain Path Press
187 West Line St, Suite 130
Bishop, CA 93514
(888) 224-9997

www.MountainPathPress.com
email: Info@MountainPathPress.com

Quantity discounts are available on bulk purchases of this book.

Also by Rick Sanger & Carol Russell:
"Are There BEARS Here?"

Special thanks to all those who made this book possible, including
Dianna Winslow, Cathy Hardin, Jim Cahill, Amy Lacefield,
and my fine and patient friends at June Mountain Ski Resort.

Publisher's Cataloging-in-Publication
(Provided by Quality Books, Inc.)

Sanger, Rick.
    Do teddy bears ski? / Rick Sanger ; Carol Russell, illustrator. -- 1st ed.
    p. cm.
    SUMMARY: Before learning to ski, a child asks his teddy bear about the ski-
ing customs of animals, and Teddy tells him some amazing tall tales about skiing tigers, porcupines, fish, etc. Appended with tips for parents who want to
teach their children to ski.
    LCCN: 98-67166
    ISBN: 0-9653149-1-X

    1. Skiing--Juvenile fiction. 2. Animals--Juvenile fiction.   I. Russell, Carol. II
Title.

PZ8.3.S2255Do 1998   [E]
                               QBI98-1524

For my dad,
Seventy-five years skiing the slopes of life
and I've yet to see him snowplow
-RS

For Nathan and Claire

who know the fun
of playing in the snow
-CR

"Hey, Mr. Teddy,
   would you please tell me,
what I will learn
   when I learn how to ski?"

"Do deer wear ski boots
    with buckles and straps,
that clamp to their skis
    with a loud sounding *snap!?*"

"And how about birds...
        do they tire of migration,
and stay north for the winter
        to ski in formation?"

"Do mice like the moguls,
the steeps, and the bumps...

Do they fly off small dimples,
         'cause for them, they're huge jumps?"

Teddy smiled at his friend,
    "Here's what I know.
It's what my pals learned
    having fun on the snow."

"Martens dress to stay warm,
        it's well worth the hassle,
five jackets, four mittens,
        and a hat with a tassel."

"Since the sun is so bright,
        and the snow is so white,
egrets wear shades
        to protect their eye sight."

"Giraffes love fresh powder,
    deep and fluffy - it's neat!
They say, 'It's like flying
    when you can't see your feet!'"

"Now, tigers are tough,
they don't have any fear,
they don't need to use poles
in order to steer."

"When bunnies fall down
        they laugh right out loud.
If they bounce up by themselves,
        it makes them feel proud."

Porcupine says,
      "It's too much uphill!
I keep slipping backwards,
      try what I will."

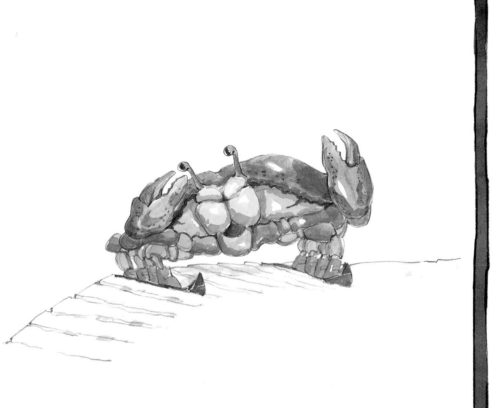

Crab knows how to do it.
    He tells him the trick.
"Just go sideways like me,
    to make your skis stick."

"To slow down, just make pizza,
    it's all you need know.
The bigger the slice,
    the slower you go!"

"I once knew a fish
        who told quite a tale,
'bout cross-country skiing
        where you make your own trail."

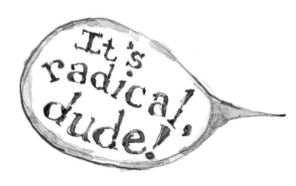

"Ruby is rad,
        she shreds like a pro.
She can't snowboard enough,
        just look at her go!"

"My friends and I love it,
it's great, we agree.
And now it is *your* turn
to learn how to ski!"

Taking Kids Skiing:
Hints for a great trip!

These tips are compiled from professionals whose lives center around teaching kids how to ski. Use them to help make your child's first ski trip as enjoyable as possible... for you *and* for them!

The Environment:

- Always use sun block! The sun is stronger at high altitudes and the snow reflects its rays so that they strike us from above and below. Sunburn can occur even on overcast days.
- Make sure your child wears sunglasses or goggles. Goggles are great for overcast or stormy days, but will fog-up and are uncomfortable on sunny, warm days. On these days, give your child sunglasses instead. Beware, some cheaper sunglasses do not block ultra-violet light (worse than wearing no sunglasses at all!).
- Some kids want to ski on days when you can't imagine leaving your seat by the lodge fireplace. If visibility is decreased due to blowing snow, consider hiring a guide or ski instructor who knows the area well. Cover all exposed skin, especially cheeks and noses to reduce the risk of frostbite. Goggles and neck gaiters are great for this.
- Dress your child in several thin layers, rather than one thick jacket. In this way, layers can be added or removed until he or she is most comfortable.
- Many children (and adults!) feel the effects of mountain elevations for the first day or two of a trip. Headaches and dizziness are common symptoms. Arriving at the ski area a day in advance will help the natural acclimatization process, as will drinking lots of water. Refrain from immediate vigorous activity; it can make the effects of altitude worse.

The Equipment:

- Hats, gloves, goggles, jackets, ski poles, and even skis are easily misplaced or mixed up with other children's belongings. Label your child's gear for easy identification. Croakies® can prevent sunglasses from being lost. Small cords with clips on the ends are available to clip hats to collars and gloves to cuffs so that if one of these items is dropped, it will stay attached to your child.
- Consider obtaining your child's skis in advance. Have him or her walk around a little in their boots, and even in their skis (first just one, then both). This familiarization will go a long way on the big day. Beware! Children will often swing skis wildly when they first wear them in an effort to walk and turn. Give them plenty of room for this experiment!
- Scarfs and chair lifts don't mix! Neck gaiters are just as warm and won't get caught in passing objects.
- Helmets are now recommended by many professionals. Often, they can be rented at the ski area. Call ahead and ask.

Safety, Fun, Learning, in that order! These are the priorities of the Professional Ski Instructors of America (PSIA). It is a good list for us all to remember!

- It is not wise to push your child beyond his or her comfort level. After all, creating happy memories is what it is all about. Besides being dangerous, rushing your child into steep terrain will force him or her into a large wedge (snowplow) instead of promoting more desirable turning skills.
- For the same reasons, don't be persuaded by an ambitious child into moving into terrain for which he or she is not ready.

- Skiing with your child between your legs is dangerous for you and him or her. This arrangement can cause you to damage a knee, and/or fall on your child. The use of a leash or Edgie Wedgie® is a better way to keep your child skiing under control. (An Edgie Wedgie is a device that keeps the ski tips together, thus facilitating a wedge.)

- Ski areas are often crowded and confusing. Consider writing your child's name and your local address on a piece of paper and putting it in his or her pocket in case he or she should become separated from you. Arrange a meeting place in the lodge for emergencies (the customer service desk is a good choice). Point out the uniformed ski instructors and other staff as safe people to talk to if your child should need help.

- At age 4, most children are ready to learn to ski. A ski lesson from a trained instructor is a great idea. Why not let an experienced professional teach proper technique from the very start? Consider taking a lesson yourself; a little bit goes a long way toward making the sport easier and more enjoyable. Enjoy some runs afterwards and show each other what you've learned!
  - Many young children have a difficult time leaving their parents behind to join a ski class. Arriving at the ski area a day early might help by giving your child a chance to see other kids having fun in classes. Ski instructors have been trained to capture a child's interest and attention as quickly as possible, but it is difficult for *any* instructor to keep a child's attention with a parent present. If you'd like to enjoy the unique scene of watching your child learning to ski in a class, please do so at a distance!

Happy Skiing! -RS

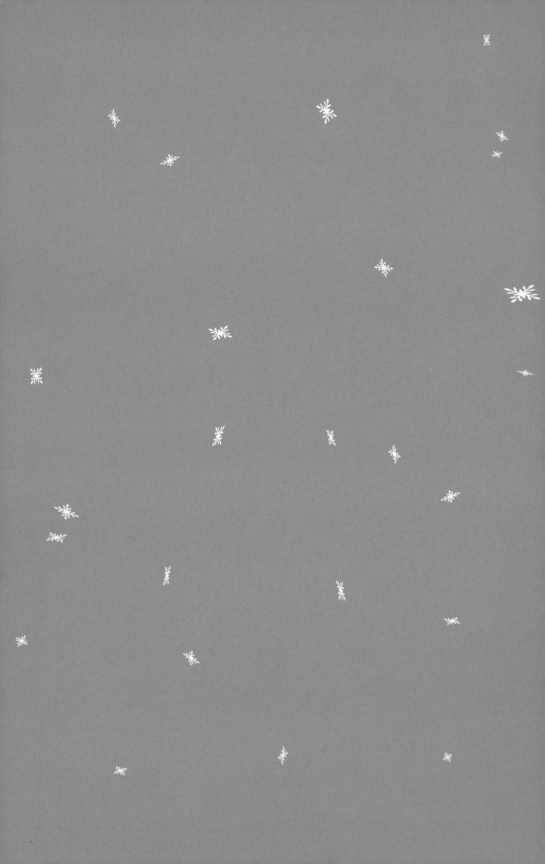